By Abir Khan

Made with ❤ on the Notion Press Platform

www.notionpress.com

# Contents

# Foreword

***

**Fantasies** is a book written by a young boy, named Abir Meraj Khan. He is currently studying in $6^{th}$ grade in Utpal Shanghvi Global School. This is Abir's second book, first being A**utobiographies.** Abir is an avid reader and aims to enter the field of medicine and become an ophthalmologist. However, he is quite interested in reading different fiction genres and has a burning desire to become a young author too. Abir, as a person is very imaginative and creative in his ideas. While writing **Fantasies** he wanted to pour his heart out, on paper. As a child he has penned down the sincerest thoughts and his understanding of the world. I hope his friends, children of his age group, young adults and even elders can relate to his ideas. He aspires to win over everyone's heart with yet another piece of writing.

Abir Khan

6th Grade Utpal Shanghvi Global School

4th February 2024.

# Acknowledgements

Gratitude, to my respected Principal, Mrs. Rakhi Mukherjee, my respected Supervisor, Mrs. Srilata Shashikumar, my valued teachers and my dear companions of Utpal Shanghvi Global School, Juhu, Mumbai.

# Prologue

*In a realm where dreams entwine with reality, where magic hums in every whisper of the wind, embark upon a journey through the rainbow of imagination. This is a world where reality and imaginations meet at the horizon, and forgotten spells await the touch of a willing heart. Welcome to an orbit where every tale is a key to unlock the door to untold wonders.*

# Chapter

# One

# Mom's Spies

# Mom's Spies

Mom planned for a home makeover and this time I was getting my own room. That meant- a little freedom. By little, I actually meant very little. Freedom to stay up late without they knowing, freedom to use my phone whenever I wish, freedom to be myself and freedom from the autocratic rules of my mom. I was content. My room was upstairs and mom put a neon sign that read **`Abir's Den'**

My room was an amalgamation of blue and green. It had posters of football players all over. Mom knew I wanted a bunk bed and there it was! It was as cosy as a bird's nest. There were night lamps for my fervent reading, attached study desk down the bunk and my wardrobe. The spotlights on my childhood photographs stole the show.

Coming to my desk, there was a Feng Shui bowl with cyan gel balls in it. Quite an unusual embellishment in my space! And that was not all, there were two figurines- one of a boy and the other of a

girl. "Interesting!" I said to myself. I found them quite amusing and I called them Cheenu and Meenu. Cheenu,

the boy, wore a yellow hat, a green jacket and blue trousers. He held a newspaper in his hand. Meenu wore a pink jacket and a blue skirt, holding a letter sealed by a heart.

Festivities were round the corner and from nowhere, a few kins teleported to our newly renovated dwelling. It was a Sunday and too chaotic to study. Suddenly, Cheenu's newspaper started to blink in red light. I was scared as if it would explode! A note flew out from it which read- **Geography Surprise Test Tomorrow**. It was kind of weird but I had a Geography lecture the next day. It was quite probable to have a test as I knew Riddhi Ma'am loved giving surprises.

I ran through the chapter, and was more or less prepared. And guess what? The test took place. The next day, after the test, the heart on Meenu's envelope started blinking and she flung a note towards me- **Geography Test- 5/5**. This was bizarre! Totally fantastical! It now became my daily routine to look for updates from Cheenu in the morning

and for results from Meenu, in the afternoon.

Mulling over these episodes, I thought I was becoming a superstitious fool. To put the whole thing to test, I decided to sleep with my parents one night. The next day, before school, I tried really hard and avoided the sight of the figurines and departed only to reveal that there was a sudden science viva at school and I had done atrociously. **My marks were 1/5**.

The moment I disclosed my marks to my mother, she verbally bashed me left, right and centre. Believe it or not, it was the duo helping me like the elves in the shoemaker's case. I surrendered to them. I looked into their eyes. They were gloomy. As if, saying, I, being their friend did not believe them. I gestured for forgiveness and apologised. Their faces lit up. A wave of happiness spread over their faces. I repented for not having trusted them. The heart on Meenu's envelope blinked. She flung a note again- **'We are friends'**

The two of them are surely a blessing in disguise to me as I didn't tag along anyone to tell me what I had to study, I am quite grateful to them as they portray me as a very responsible and an efficient personality.

# Chapter Two

# A Day out with Roach

# A Day out with Roach

We all must have heard that cockroaches can survive in any condition and they lived way before human existence. They could fly and tread on water! Navratri, being round the corner, our society compound was on a '**Cleanliness Drive**'. All hidden lairs were exposed. Right from those of the mice to those of lizards. An enormous infestation of cockroaches was out with a gush of water flooding into their cloister. Unaware of the asepsis, my family and I were heading to the mall and with no whiff a cockroach snuck into our car.

Well, I do not suffer from **entomophobia**, but my mum does. I decided to rather be

quite and let the mini beast creep out unnoticed. I closed my eyes on the backseat and went into another world with this petite monster. I was the same size as this being. I befriended him! Apparently, he was so fluent with English that I actually felt, if he wouldn't be a cockroach, he could be a journalist as a human. I wanted to be with **Roach**, only to improve my English. He, too, found me too inferior to him. Not because my English wasn't up to the mark, because I couldn't fly. Well, both the arts were to my advantage, so I preferred his company. Just imagine! I wanted to take English lessons from a pest!

Very **proactively**, he started teaching me how to fly. I wondered how would that be possible. Living with the being, I was actually getting **structurally adapted** to the surroundings I wandered with him. Soon I mastered the art of gliding in the air. I actually felt I was quite quirky!

As a pal of the cockroach, we had no permanent address. We somehow landed in a very aromatic precinct. Warm and always smelling of something sweet. The enclosure was quite hueful. We saw something like a white bed balancing a rainbow on it. Awesome! It was a scrumptious **Rainbow cake**! It tickled

everything in me. More than eating it, I wanted to play in the bed of cream and slide on the colourful arc.

It was nightfall and pitch dark. Both our **nocturnal** modes were turned on. Roach read my mind and in our prankishness, at the drop of a hat, clambered to the summit of the spectrum and slid, topsy-turvy. Each time we landed on the white cream, we were smeared in it with our mouths full with its sweetness. We were slipping, sliding, plodding and falling to our heart's content. "it is so much fun being a cockroach", I gleefully uttered.

But then, from nowhere, a **villain** arrived! It was a worker who picked us up by our antennae and tossed us out of the window. Huge beings are actually very cruel and insensitive. "I go through this almost every time I'm caught by most of the courageous women in their **kitchen**," Roach said smiling at me.

Roach, then invited me to his territory. Although, I knew it would be yucky but that goon's death stare was frightening! We went down a steep, perpendicular wall into a dark well. The milieu was quite spine-chilling. Our voices echoed. Though having the nocturnal traits, I couldn't figure out anything. Roach uttered something- it wasn't English.

And all of a sudden, I was surrounded by a million other species in the debris. The place was stinky and claustrophobic. However, the place was, the others, too, were amiable and hospitable. They offered me a whole buffet of all what they had- a dead fly, a smelly piece of paper, fungal bread piece, awful mucky drinks and what not. Good, that I had Roach as my saviour or else I would die of stuffing.

Even though their life style was disgusting, their intention and kindness was something that was respectable. I was trying to take French leave, suddenly, I felt a jerk at my knees. When I opened my eyes, we had reached the mall. Roach was nowhere to be seen. I guess I'd dropped him to safety among his brood members.

# Chapter Three

# A Banana Rescue

# A Banana Rescue

Today, was Independence Day for me, as it was **A Parents' Day Out**! Study (my canine) and I were **Home Alone**. It was our first time when we were going to be by ourselves. By 9.00 a.m. the two of them were already on the way to their picnic spot. I already knew what I was up to, the moment they would step out of the house-

**Bath bombs**

As I set foot in the bathroom, the slimy flooring pushed me right into the bath tub, as if it was longing to start the fun with the contents in my hand.

The touch of water crumbled them into a thousand pieces and in no time the whole bathroom was frothing. I could do nothing as all five of them dissolved instantly. Study and I were completely hidden, in and behind the huge froth mountains. Study, somehow, is hydrophobic, but here, she was enthralled. I felt some small plastic, spongy, rod-like objects under my buttocks. I wondered what they were? Suddenly, they blew up! And out came yellow balloons with glasses. I gaped at it and it stared back at me, blinking heavily.

It was a living minion! Study too was dumbstruck at the sight of this single-eyed yellow creature. Again, I felt a push on my left palm that was resting on the tub floor. Another minion popped up from the soapy water in a huge wave. Study, all of a sudden, jumped as, yet another minion was right behind her and in no time we were spotting sudden eruption from every corner of the bathroom.

I huddled out, uncovered, feeling

shamelessly nude. Study and the mob of minions started barking at each other, as if competing, who was louder. One of them from nowhere started **straightening her tail**. It felt like they had never seen a dog, and, got bitten by her.

All of them pounced at her at once.

Everything was in helter-skelter and all

of us were running haphazardly. The minions were so hungry that they turned the house upside-down, looking for bananas- even in the commodes. They were so famished!

After a while, I was drained and the house was in total discord and cacophony. "Shut up you hooligans!" I howled at them as if I was a monitor of an undisciplined class. They all stood stunned in to silence. "At once, I want all of you to settle on the couch. And remember! Not a word. Do you all get it. Not a word!" They all looked terrified. In spite of instructing them to be on the couch, due to space crunch, they all sprawled all over the house. Even on the bed where I wanted to let loose myself. They promised to bring the house to harmony. I must say they looked so innocent and **angel-like** with those puppy faces after such a harsh scolding that I started feeling sorry for them. But what about the mess?

Well, it had all started with me but I had no clue how it reached to that an extent.

In no time, all of them were snoring away to glory. And the funniest part was somehow, Study and I adjusted ourselves amidst the clutter, but we were royally kicked out of our own bed. There was not a piece of land in our own house to rest our butts. Anyways, after an hour's uneasy nap, I shook one of them, who looked like the **Minion Leader** to wake him up. He started whimpering his lungs out- like a baby.

Mulling over how to deal with this cry baby and the mess all over, the doorbell rang abruptly. All the other minions, started crying in one voice. I actually started tearing my hair upurl. It was mom, standing right up there. At the entrance. I had lost my capacity to cope with another tantrum, but before that she fainted. I actually thanked God for that and there from behind the turn, my rescuer came into sight- my father.

The Jing bang peered at him and in a jiffy pounced on his shoulders and snatched the plastic bag of bananas that he was holding. Mom lay sprawled on the floor with Study licking her face to bring her to consciousness. "What's going on Abir? Where did you encounter them?" Dad's desperate voice resounded. "Long story dad! Not now! Let's face the mayhem!"

Dad threw the bananas at the throng and ran down stairs. I lifted mom and rested her on the couch. I had no clue what dad was up to, the way he chased away leaving me stranded in the muddle. A few of them followed him as if they wanted to bite him. From the window I even spotted him lifting these yellow monsters. He had sprinted to the fruit stall. I got it! "Bananas!" I screamed and ran towards dad. They all flowed like yellow water behind me. We somehow, managed all of them out of the building compound and got them busy, eating.

Dad pushed me out amongst them and we locked the high compound gates and sneaked away. What a day! And what an escapade! Dad sprinkled water on mom's face to bring her to senses. Looking at the condition of the house, she fainted again!

# Chapter
# Four

# A Secret Unveiled

# A Secret Unveiled

During our formative years in school, I want you to recollect about what all we've learnt about clouds. Basically, how they are formed in the process of water cycle? Or their types- Cirrus, Cumulonimbus, Cumulus, Stratus, etc. However, have you ever guessed, sometimes, why do we see a soufflé in the form of a duck. Perhaps, people send video of a cluster of clouds forming a silhouette of Ganapati- our elephant-headed God!

Well, have you ever wondered why clouds form different shapes. Yeah,

yeah, as they are blown by the wind, they merge into each other und appear to form different shapes. And we relate them to the most familiar object that is known to us. I am one kind of a person, who loves to look into emptiness. And very often, you may find me gaping at a stone or a huge rock on a beach. Or

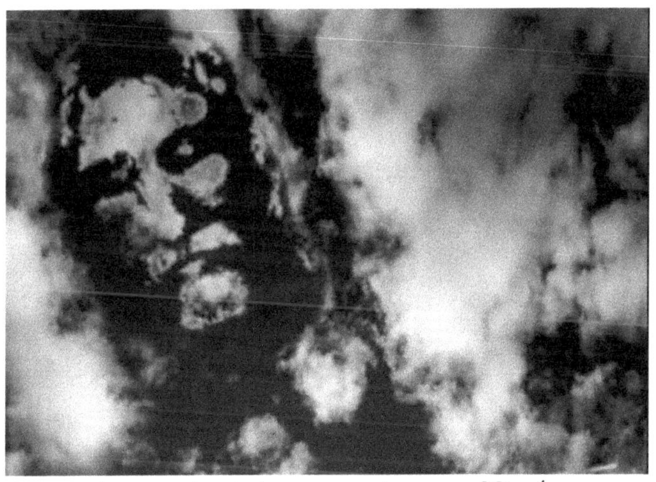

sometimes, looking at the traffic jam, from my terrace, on the busy street adjacent to my house.

Interestingly, all these clutters and clusters form different contours as a whole. Very randomly, I may figure out a dog or Jesus or a simple smiley in the sky and start pondering if it is some kind of a message or indication from the **Creator** for me?

One such odd evening, Mum and I decided to go for a jog to the nearby park. I must tell you, I love going there. Every space out there, has something interesting going on. It has a walking track on which you will see all the stylish youngsters and not so young, jogging or brisk walking, in their latest fitness outfits and exorbitant shoes. Their classy bottles and their wristbands are one of a kind. Their sweaty, red faces and their determination to burn out is exhilarating.

In one circular portion you can see a gang of senior citizens, catching up with each other on latest updates of gossips and some sincerely trying to maintain their laughter club. If you sit and observe them keenly, you actually can start laughing on nothing. I like to call them '**back to toddling club**'. Their no reason laughter and their way of noticing others and trying to get a hold of them touches my soul.

Then in another zone, is a skating rink. Children and teenagers swaying and wheeling, talking to the winds, trying various stunts, enjoying themselves to the fullest, or may be, practising for a tournament. These young champions are exuberant! Fully charged! Overflowing with energy and emanating.

In one corner, you will see the actual tots sliding and swinging delightfully with their parents. That corner is certainly the noisiest of all with all children merrily chuckling and calling out to one another.

And last, but not the least, the vast expanse of lush green grass, which is the real beauty of the place, outlined by hedges of bushes contained with flowers of pulchritudinous hues.

So, we were here- at the park. Mum and I, jogging, looking around and greeting our acquaintances. I wondered how others must be looking at us- judging us by our clothing or not carrying a fancy sipper. Well, Mum hardly cared. But, by now, you must have guessed, I noticed- no one cared about the other. After, around five laps we decided to sit on the green carpet (the grass).

Soon, I being me, starting looking at the butterflies fluttering on the blossoms. What I noticed is, that they moved in a very random motion. They never landed in a straight path on a particular flower. First, they hovered over it, went in different directions and then, gently landed on them. But why did they do so? Did they play around among themselves, something like musical chairs and then gently sat on their choice or was it that they were grabbing the flowers attention to allow them to be their companion.

Apparently, that could never be figured out until, someone spoke to them. But all I was trying to find out how they moved about, so, I started tracing my fore finger on their path of movement. It was jumbling! Mum was speaking to her friend and her son who was watching me, suspected that I was a maniac, a nut of some kind. He had an art kit on his shoulder. I quickly pulled him in a jerk and abruptly unzipped his bag to pull out his art book and a pencil.

Both the ladies were muddled at my behaviour and the little son definitely was now vexed. I didn't care. All I cared was to trace the path of one of the butterflies. I held the book page vertically and clearly trailed the pattern on the paper.

It made no sense to me nor to the others watching me. Blowing out my breath heavily, I looked up into the sky. A random cloud caught my sight. Now, I was holding the doodling against the sky. They matched. I was soon following the road of another flutter and correlated it with another fluffle. This time it was a bunny rabbit on the paper as well as, in the clouds.

Mum and aunt were sure that I was crazy and the little kid snatched away his book and pencil from me, attempting to scratch me. But, never mind. I had an amazing revelation for Mum.

I felt I unveiled the ways almighty shaped his clouds- sometimes that made sense to me and sometimes it did not. But whenever I went to the park I definitely watched the butterflies and the clouds in sync with each other.

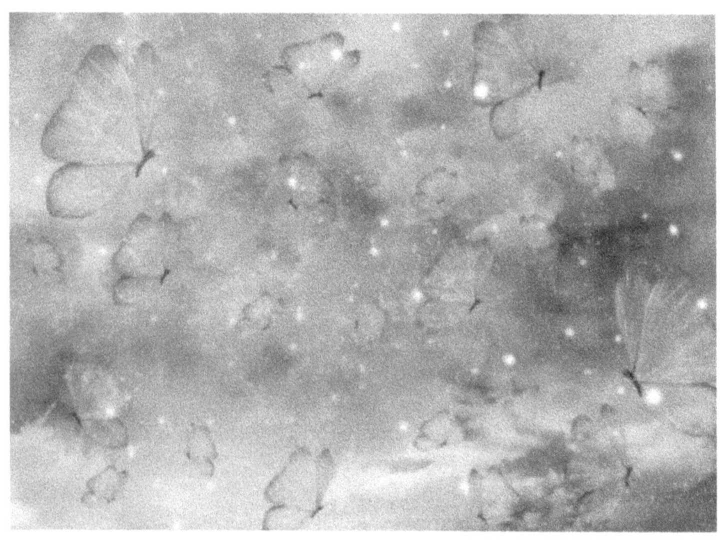

# Chapter

# Five

# God Will Smile Soon

# God Will Smile Soon

I've always got lessons on humanity, humble behaviour and kindness from my folks at home. The women in my family believe in selfless love and unselfish efforts for all beings. All of them have brought up my brother and me to believe in signs from **Mother Nature** and **The Protector**.

We have a female dog. Her name is **Study**. My brother, so influenced by my mother's preaching, heartfully feels that she is a blessing too. Even if she bites us, and our wounds are profusely bleeding, she's yet not scolded upon and we dare not even frown at her. They take her to be an angel. A dog- angel? Do they fantasize that she has wings and there is a magic wand or some sort attached to her tail?

Here, on looking our living room, we have a small aesthetic garden. The flowerbed has a Rose plant, a Bougainvillea, a Cherry tomato and hybrid Orange Bonsais. I thought my granny likes them for their colourful appearance and ornamental value. But no! She had another set of sentiments attached to them. If we stayed home over the weekend, we too used to start thinking in her fashion. But by the time it was Wednesday, we had our own doubts.

Our women, lead an extremely simple life with fantasies attached to everything around, and, as a child, I too love to believe their beliefs. So, the ornamental garden is being nurtured by my granny. Every time, a Rose blossoms in there, she calls out to me, taking a check if I had done a good deed or perhaps I've not lied or I've stood up for the right. Her thought behind it is that, it's God's own way of rewarding us and encouraging us to do these little good things and this is how **He** appreciates us. She always says, "God is happy with you and he's smiling because of you in the form of a blossom."

But since a few days, she is acting a bit selfish, saying that it is not my good deed that God is smiling upon, it is hers. "If you want Bappa to be happy with you, plant your own Rose." Well, it always pleases me to look at the little garden. And now, in her own way she's insisting on me planting a new life. I actually planted one. In about three weeks, I saw the new one germinate and take form. I can see thorns on its branches and I'm hoping at least a couple of them would bud soon. But I'm quite sure I will find a blooming Rose only if I made a good gesture towards humanity soon.

# Chapter

# Six

# Ballerina

# Ballerina

Sometimes life can be so monotonous. I'm sure many of us just drag along the sluggish week- those five days of school, with the same old sessions of Maths, Science, History and so on. And so often, I have those **Monday Blues** after the weekends. Relatable? Or am I the only one?

All of a sudden on Sunday, after dinner, when I was packing my bag, according to the schedule for the next day, it clicked that Mrs. Iyer, our maths teacher, had called for our Geometry boxes. I scurried down to the stationery and desperately demanded for one. The shop keeper barely had some decent colour options. He had a pink

coloured Barbie box and one purple box. I had no other option but to pick up the witch's colour. I was sure my friends in school would have a hearty laugh, the moment I would bring the box out of my sack.

The day at school was as normal as it could be. Malini Ma'am had given us loads of practice sheets as we all had butter fingers. Trust me, not a single one amongst us could hold a ruler in place as the pencil slid against it. Manviraj, my friend, the clumsiest of all, was sure to win a gold medal in the pencil-dropping competition if someone held one. Every time she heard the pencil falling, she turned towards him and tore her hair out. My poor friend, all he did was made a puppy face to escape our ma'am's wrath.

Post lunch, Mom and I sat down to do the practice sheets. The bunch consisted of sheets on drawing line segments, angles, triangles and circles. In no time, I finished the easier ones, but for me, making arc and circles was a challenge. I guess I had two left hands. Every time I would try to swirl my compass, it would slip out of my fingers. Cynically, my Mum put a

Barbie eraser on the pencil that was held in the clamps of the compass, "Now imagine the pencil dancing like a ballerina." Really? Had she lost her marbles? "You dare not pull the eraser out", she screamed and walked off to grab a cup of coffee. The next statement on the sheet said, 'Draw a circle with a radius of 3 cm'.

I pulled the hands of the compass apart, measured it on the ruler, fixed the point

of the steel hand on the page and twisted the pencil on the paper. I drew a line from the point on the page to the edge of the circle.

Mom measured it. Yessss! It was correct. "Can I remove the eraser now?" I asked. She nodded. My next one was a circle with a 10cm diameter. This time I did the same thing that I had done earlier, but the compass slipped out of my hand again.

My Mum was now disgusted. I quietly put the eraser back onto the pencil thinking that Mom's facial expressions would soften to a slight crescent smile. I attempted to draw the circle again. Apparently, I saw a ballerina twirl for the 5cm radius circle. Now, each time I drew an arc for the triangles or a circle or a geometric design in my art lecture I could imagine a ballerina dancer with a bun on her head, secured with a lavender ribbon, clad in a short outfit, moving in circles on her toes. Was she the reason for my Geometry going right or is it my imagination? Does this dancing doll actually glide on the paper or is it that I have wild imaginations? Nonetheless, my figures are drawn correctly by me? Or the Barbie eraser? Whatever be it, I'm not going to get the eraser off my pencil. At least, not in my examination answer sheet.

# Chapter Seven

# Illustrations

# Illustrations

If people enjoy drawing and painting, art and colours, then, an art lecture can be very soothing to the mind. Especially, if it is the first hour at school. Your power of visualizing objects and scenes can make you travel all around the Universe and beyond. I am a football freak, and I tend to be very aggressive on field. Somewhere, shading and stroking on the paper pacifies me.

I've always found Warli to be a brilliant art form- simple and elegant. Without the use of colours, it evolves as a master piece. Just imagine, if a painter pours hues in it, what will it come out to be! I've always seen myself wandering on the canvas, in a beautiful village adorned by thatched huts, coconut trees

and sailing in the wooden boat. Well, in one of the Warli drawings, I totally got engrossed.

I had been to the library and running my eyes over the bookshelves, my gaze halted on this book titled **'Hole-and-Corner-Warli'**. I was curious. I pulled it out from the middle of the other books only to see it was made by an anonymous person. Strange! Wasn't it? It had a black cover with a white arrow with a red tip. As if it was blood-stained.

A subdued voice from within me called out to hold back. But I couldn't. My palms started sweating as the book felt spooky and paranormal. I opened the book to the first illustration. The figures in the pictures were moving. It appeared as if the human figures in it were trying to hide. I flipped the page. The next one displayed glimpses of fifteen of them being killed by a few attackers. I went into a disturbed frame of mind. A part of me begged not to continue with the book, but the other screamed that these villagers needed help.

I flipped a few more pages and gained that this book was about the village called **Katkariwadi**, located in the interiors of Maharashtra. The villagers were in constant terror of attacks. The sun rays and water were a treat to them. They had locked themselves up in lairs unknown as they faced danger of life, the moment they faced the Sun. The pictures narrated the schmaltz of how people survived. I wept at the sight of all what I saw and when I looked up there was no one around me in the library.

My heart was doleful. I kept the book back from where I had picked it up. The scenes haunted me all the way back home. I wanted to cry my heart out. I grieved. Next day was School again. I ran up to the library to find the book. I couldn't. I inquired with our library teacher, Mrs. Sarla. She confirmed that there was no such book in our library. I frantically held her hand and showed her where I had picked it up from. She yet stuck to what she had affirmed. I went up daily, for the next two weeks, to check if someone had returned it, but in vain. Sarla ma'am reassured that there was no such book.

I looked up the net, I even visited the popular libraries in town, but all I was informed that no such book was available with them.

In another month's time I lost hope that I would find it and the story that I framed looking at the illustrations were all my own fantasies. Then, all of a sudden, I heard our Principal, Mrs. Mukherjee announcing that our school had adopted the village called Katkariwadi and we all had to come up in service for a sustainable development. I was baffled. My thoughts ran down back to the book. I pleaded to my father to actively participate in the programme and that we should all visit the place once.

Dad refused. I had no way to dig deeper and find out, what I had known about the village was true or false.

Being a regular visitor to the library, hunting for a decent book to read, this time, I again came across the same book. The moment I turned around to show it to our library teacher, I realised that I was alone in there. Not a teacher around, not a student in there. I quickly flipped a few more pages and read the pictures that told me how Savni, a brave eight-year-old girl, had saved the village by poisoning the only water well, from where the attackers quenched their thirst. Believing in her courage, her parents too actively executed the plot.

Savni and her family had rescued the village from the attackers but could not help the villagers from dying of thirst and starvation. I closed the book, headed to the Principal's office to find out the real story behind the adoption. However, our principal ma'am was right before me while I was sprinting down the staircase. I wanted to know the real reason behind the good deed. All she explained to me, "The reason behind it is unknown to all of us, however, I want students not to doubt us in anyway and support the sustenance programme". From within, how I wanted to tell her the story that I had known and how strongly I wanted to be a part of every bit of the programme, but I uttered nothing.

Well, God has his own ways of sending angels for help to the needy and here I feel, Mrs. Mukherjee's drive for the cause would save the village from all adversities.

# Chapter Eight

# A Quintuple Trip

# A Quintuple Trip

Have you ever taken a ride in a double decker bus? Have you seated yourself on the first seat where there are two huge windows- one in front of you and the other on the side? What a feel, sitting on the first storey of a moving bus and the driver under you, suddenly brakes, speedily moves through all the twists and turns of the narrow lanes of Mumbai! The bumps on the breakers, the jerks that push you forward actually gives me goose bumps.

But the excitement too, is on another level. You feel you are the king of the world. I sometimes imagine myself as a courageous warrior, mounted on an elephant's back, fearlessly marching to conquer a fort. By now, you must have understood how my imaginations run, with no head and no tail.

So, here, in broad day light, I start fantasizing, being on a quintuple (five) decker bus. I am sitting on the first seat, in front of the enormous window and the bus is moving steadily. The vehicle had an elevator. A glass elevator. I went up, dashing through the transparent walls, huddling myself to the front edge. I only wondered how did the driver balance the floors on wheels.

As I comforted myself on the front seat, I realized that I could take a peak into the roadside houses whose curtains and windows were wide open. Some, where I could see ladies cooking, while in some I saw a huge television screening a cricket match. While I was on the trip, I completely forgot about my existence on this quintuple. As if I was viewing rushes of a movie.

Soon, I could see a road signal. It was red and the bus felt as if it was at a speed of 60km/hour. I was not sure of the driver's skills. How was he planning to bring the vehicle to a halt at such a short distance? Why was he at such a high speed in the middle of such busy streets of a metropolitan city? Didn't he care that there were people sitting on higher floors and if he braked suddenly, people would ram against the front walls of the bus?

I was scared. My front window was open. Luckily, the colour changed and the bus did not even have to slow down. I was safe, but not going to be always. Instead of enjoying the cool breeze, the sight from that height and the experience, I was fearing the next halt. At that speed, I felt like a caterpillar dangling from one side of a springy branch, who would be thrown out of the window any moment.

I wanted to hold on to my seat tightly, but it had no handles. The driver now was speeding up, over 60 km/hour, in circles, along an S-shaped route, dashing through the buildings. I thought of going down to him, but our bus was racing. I still walked down, clenching the pillars, balancing myself.

To my horror, the driver was fast asleep. The bus was driving itself. I leapt to the seat. I could hear yells and cries from people on the bus. I was on the driving seat. That meant, the safety of a lot of lives was in my hands. I did not lose the power to think. I decided to gradually decelerate. I watched the speedometer thoroughly in intervals of seconds. It came down from 80 to 75, then to 70 in time spans of ten seconds each.

A signal again. I was horrified! I was definitely going to meet with an accident. To avoid striking into something, I turned the steering wheel and was soon running on an empty road, something like a sea link. Phew! My armpits were wet, my throat was parched and my fingers were glued to the steering wheel. I again started slowing down. Here, on this track it was safe. I had managed to bring down the pace to 50 km/hour. The driver was still sleeping away to glory. I yelled at everyone to grip on to anything that would keep them safe.

I had, by now, brought down the speed to 20 km/ hour and somewhere was happy with the course of my doing. I really didn't know even now when could I step on the brake, which I did skeptically. We were at 0 km/hour, finally we all were safe. Trust me, this dream of mine haunts me several times in the morning of being on a towering bus like this. I prefer waking up and distracting myself from such a fantasy every time.

# Chapter Nine

# Paara

# Paara

In the fifth grade, our fiction topic for the term was **Legends**. We were told to read a lot about Greek Mythology. All about Zeus, Hercules, Apollo and many others.

Reading one such story, **'The Gorgons' Head'** gave me a glimpse about Quicksilver. Just by reading a few sentences about him, I found him to be a magnetic personality. I read a mention of him even in the tale of **'Pandora's Box'**. Well, from that day on, I took him to be quite a cool dude. I started hunting for his sketches on the internet. A well-built guy with a muscular body, a radiant, chiselled face, a smile with dimples- well, they were all in my head.

All that I found in his sketches were, a shaft that had a pair of snakes coiling

up, his winged sandals and his loose T-shirt with shorts (that's what I think I can call it). His toned thighs and calves could be an absolute delight for body builders.

I wondered if I could meet him some day... And I did... as you know me...

I had been to this place called Shvas Island based in Igatpuri. The drive up there was quite steep and it was not meant for driving. The roads to reach up to the hotel were muddy, dusty and bumpy. Somehow, we reached our destination. It was a lush green place with cottages that looked over the Vaitarna Lake. A narrow, steep flight of stairs, made of cemented tiles, descended down to the lake. We were surrounded by trees of all kinds.

Gazing at the beauty of nature, amidst the hues of the precinct, I spotted a lean guy, wheatish, wearing a band around his head, a mud-stained T-shirt and holding a crooked stick. He was quite engrossed in the ripples that were being formed every time a fish came to the surface. Looked like each one of them rose up to greet him. None of the others

in my family noticed him. We stayed there for a while, clicked a few snaps and headed to our room.

Our balcony, was just above the water and far in the distance we could see another small island adorned with a bijou cottage in white and red, surrounded by a handful of coconut trees. I notice the same lad, rowing his boat to the other end of the water. Though he was an unattractive guy, there was something that always drew my attention to him.

The next morning, while all were drowned in their beds, I was wide awake at the crack of dawn. I decided to walk out of the room stealthily into the mist of the air, feeling the dew on the grass on my feet. I decided to walk up to the same place where we had clicked a dozens of snaps. At the wee hours, I again noticed the same guy, feeding the fishes. I decided to befriend him. "Hi! I'm Paara", he introduced himself. As he smiled at me, his dimples dug into his cheeks. He shook hands with me. I could feel the strength in his arms and as I delved, he was quite a nature lover. "The birds wake me up with their chirps and the fishes call me for a swim with them every morning. The tree branches bow down to caress my face and I run behind the squirrels to chase them." He was a caring guy and offered me an apple.

Paara, somehow, figured out that I was a sports person and I told him that I passionately played my game of football. He instantly bolted towards a small enclosure and brought out a golden, glittery pair of shoes. "Here! Take these. You may need them for your future endeavours." I found them quite jazzy, yet I accepted them as he offered them to me with a lot of affection. They fitted me perfectly. As I walked to my room, wearing them, I felt quite strange. It felt as if I was gliding. I turned around to bade him goodbye as I knew I was to check out in a couple of hours and may not see him again before leaving. Paara had a divine smile spread across his face.

As I was **gliding** to my room, I saw Mum frowning at me. All of a sudden, I felt a tug at my feet and I sped to the room, the moment she turned around to go in. While packing up, sketches of Quicksilver slipped out of my backpack and lay scattered across the floor. I was reminded of Paara. His smile, his stick, the glittery shoes that I was gifted and the peculiar gait after wearing it! Were they the latest style of his winged sandals? His name was Paara, which meant Mercury in Hindi- another name for Quicksilver!

# Chapter

# Ten

# Pixie Dust

# Pixie Dust!

My said sister, Reshma di, is a teacher in our tutorial and her favourite students are the ones that belong to the **Early Years**. To lure them, and keep them glued, she sometimes makes butterflies out of origami and sometimes it snows with Styrofoam balls, to give the children an effect of winters. Sometimes she adorns their

cute faces with tiaras of flowers and leaves and sometimes she tattoos their wrists with glitter.

Glittery powder, apparently, has always fascinated me- especially the green, purple and golden ones. I relate it to pixie dust. The one that Tinker Bell had.

All of us have a few teeny-weeny lamentations. My father, grumbles about the daily traffic to work. I wish to sprinkle a little of the dust on his vehicle so that his travel to work is not so stressful. Everyday, my Mum nags over the mess created by us in the house- I want to dust the room with pixie at times for her. Many a times, my sister, Reshma, is striving with a concept that her pupils can't understand, by dusting this magical glitter on the children, I want to make it easier for her.

Life is just about daily ups and downs- sunshine and snow. With a small packet of magic, I want to see a relief on the faces of my loved ones.

It pains me, when, my friend, Yuvaan, is always standing outside Mrs. Shashikumar's office, waiting to be reprimanded. For him, I guess I would have to approach Tinker Bell for sacks and sacks of it.

O Lord! I want a day of shower- A shower of this magical powder on all of us. And all of us, sitting on our school playground, terraces, gardens and balconies being blessed with goodness, however, inappropriate our behaviour had been, Amen!

# Chapter Eleven

# The Water in My Bottle

# The Water in My Bottle

I was holding the **Guided Tour**- "Follow Your Dreams". We had a reservation at the Hong Kong Disneyland. Yippie! Father was taking me to Disneyland and I was going to have the most spectacular vacation this year.

So, here we were! We had planned our visit thoroughly so that we did not miss out on the slightest of fun. The first day, was all on the rides-enjoying the **Toy Soldier Parachute Drop, The Iron Man Experience, The RC Racer** and what not!

Day-2 was adventurous. I visited the **Festival of Lion King** and **The Magic Dreams Castle**. When I reached the **Jungle River Cruise**- I realised it was quite a place. While we set sail for high adventure, I clicked truckloads of snaps and I don't know what made me fill my bottle with the water of the untamed **River of Adventure**. I watched the playful, elephants splashing and the hefty rhinoceroses basking. It was a well spent day with lots and lots of memories to take back. Well, by dusk, we were back to our hotel. We couldn't move an inch out of the bed- we were so worn out.

On the third day, we had to check out and we were prancing towards Macau. Dad had planned some extreme sports like **Macau Tower Bungy Jump** and **Indoor Skydiving**. But just the sight from the tall towers made me feel woozy. I was asked to take a few pills, but I did not take them. Instead, I pretended, as I didn't want to encounter those daredevil feats. I uncapped my bottle and hurled those medicines in the bottle which contained the water of the River of Adventure. There was a slight fizz when the chemical came in contact with the water and I quickly screwed the cap back.

We ambled up to our room. I was still pretending to be unwell, in order to escape Dad's ire. Just then, I took a sip from my water bottle, forgetting about its contents. A loud shiver ran through my body, making my hair stand on end. I sprang up to my feet and started trumpeting imitating an elephant. I ran to the bathtub in the bathroom where my mum had pooled up the hot water for a dip. I started sucking in water through my mouth and spitting it out like a hose on everyone. My mum was horror-struck. I looked like a maniac. I scrambled back to my bed and lay down. A jerk in me and everything was back to normal. We all stood flabbergasted! I was a wild elephant.

The next morning, we were to visit a few more spots, so, I rushed for a quick shower. Before entering, I took a sip from my bottle again. Again, a huge quiver, and, this time I lay flat on the wet bathroom floor, in my shorts and sando, palms down, arms curved. I was a crocodile this time. My parents walked into the bathroom with terror, covering their eyes, looking at me through the gaps of their fingers. In a jiffy, I was back on my toes, as if nothing had happened.

My father was pretty sure that this was something to do with the water in the bottle. So, to testify it, he asked me to sip it again. "I won't do it... you have it," I protested. I didn't want to look funny again. Mum and I pushed the bottle to his lips and tilted it for him to have a swallow. He went on fours and as he spotted a plant in the room, he started taking mouthful of it. He was a zebra. The strange thing was that it was an artificial money plant.

What kind of a liquid was that? Some kind of an animal instinct potion?

# Chapter Twelve

# My Wooden Window

# My Wooden Window

All windows have an interesting world outside them; very different from what is within. My bedroom has a well-

designed wooden window, arc-shaped, opening outwards.

It has a broad parapet, where mom has placed an artificial garden in a huge bowl.

Outside the window, there were a couple of coconut trees, Ashoka trees and an Oak. Many a times, I would visualize angels sitting in a circle, chit-chatting, and their voices reached my ears. "Which house do we enter today?" I

would quickly hide behind the curtain, not to get noticed. But somewhere, deep in my heart, I always wanted them to decide upon my dwelling, and amidst all the hullabaloo, I always missed out on their choice and when I would resume my position, they were gone. How would I have a hunch of how they decided their night shelter?

Blessed is the home where angles pay a visit. But blessed are the people who see angles? On and off, I watch them on the trees- smelling flowers, playing with the little chicks in their nests, chasing caterpillars and sliding down the branches seated on a waxy leaf.

I sometimes have seen little footsteps in the miniature garden. But that's when my little cousin brings her Barbie doll and she pretend plays with her. But yesterday, she hadn't come home. Were they an angel's trail then?

# Chapter Thirteen

# Rapunzel's Hair Clip

# Rapunzel's Hair Clip

It was a gloomy day. I thought the Sun was unhappy. May be, it wanted to go on a strike. As the dark clouds capered the heavens, strong gusts made everything sway to its music. It felt like the sky started snivelling and had its own woes. Well, the glad tidings were that my table tennis class was cancelled. And the scourge was that mom asked me to tidy up my drawer. Scattering everything in my drawer, I found my photo album.

To keep the ball rolling... I started flipping through the photographs and was soon down the memory lane. I was barely five and I was reading Rapunzel with one leg on top of the other. At that age, what an arrogant manner to sit, I thought. Out of all the fairy tales, Rapunzel entranced me the most. Her captivity in the tall tower, her extra-long braid and the prince who rope climbed to meet his **friend**. Yeah... Neither of them knew initially, that they would fall in love.

Huh... I didn't want to tidy up, but I was forced to, how tyrannical... I somehow managed to do it to my mom's satisfaction but then my back started hurting and I wanted to catch forty winks.

Soon I met Rapunzel! Crying, sobbing, whimpering. What made her cry? Had the witch returned? Or, was her hair not growing that long again? After a lot of pleading, she spoke up, "I've lost my hair clip that I had to wear at the ball today. It's missing since two days." Really! A mere, paltry hair clip made the to-be queen cry? I just can't handle women crying. Gosh! "If I am not able to take care of my own things, how will I take care of my subjects, you nerd!" Well, what could I say after this. "You've vexed me terribly, and now, you will find my favourite hair clip for me," and she stormed away.

How terribly a menial job! I didn't even know how it looked. Now what- look for a needle in a haystack. I didn't know how to go about it. Perhaps, I could ask any of my female friends for help. But what would I tell them? I decided to go to her palace and ask for details to her hair dressers.

Thank God, they were helpful. Wait a minute! I had seen the similar kind of hairclip that Stud (my female dog) had picked up from the garden. Mom thought she liked it so she had clamped it in her mouth. Mom had washed it

and neatly clipped it on her fringes after she gave her a bath.

Poor Rapunzel! Stud loves her stuff immensely and I did not have the courage to be bitten by her to return her clip.

Sorry Rapunzel... You will have to go to the ball without your clip. You can sue me if you like.

# Chapter

# Fourteen

# Giving Up

# Giving Up

When I wrote my first book - **Autobiographies,** many a times I didn't know what to write or how to start. I had no plot in head. I tried really hard and

would cudgel my brains. So often, I was tired and went to sleep. There were innumerable times when I was exasperated, yet didn't come up with anything decent to write.

I almost left the idea of writing. And, on one such day, when I gave myself the last chance saying, "If not today, then never", I sat down with a lot of ideas, but I couldn't pen them down. Utterly disgusted and frustrated with myself, I left my diary open, pen open and walked into the kitchen to make myself a cup of coffee.

I had already wasted two hours, with nothing productive, hence I decided to just shut this entire affair of trying to be an author. I had my coffee, walked into my room, pulled out my Maths book and was about to set myself on my study table again.

Something very strange took place. The uncapped pen was writing in my diary. It was moving on the page. It was writing words and sentences. No hand holding the pen. I was perplexed as to what was going on. I was scared out of my wits was afraid of my own shadow now. When it finished writing, the pen comfortably lay down back on the book, as if it was just there, in that position, always.

It took me a while to digest what had just happened. When I came back to my senses and took a peek, the title of the story was '**Mother's Tales**'. I panicked. I couldn't see a hand holding the pen. The handwriting was just the same as mine. How could this be real? I started to believe that there was perhaps an invisible person in the room or may be '**Mr. India**' had jumped out of his movie.

# Chapter Fifteen

I walked up to Pandora...

# I walked up to Pandora…

Once, I walked up to Pandora. I was damn pissed off at her. I wished I could put her behind bars, take her to some isolated Indonesian Island and leave her there.

She was right in front of me, rubbing her eyes after a good sleep. She was sleeping! After giving all worries and trouble to the world, she was slumbering away to glory? She doesn't even realise what a living hell did she make for us, the children, especially studying in middle school.

The moment I saw her in this state, I yelled at her- "Who do you think you are? For your own **whims and fancies**, you've buried us in books.

Come out of your dreams and see how difficult our Maths formulae are! Come and take a look at our Marathi essays and to top it all remember dates in History. Have you ever caught a glimpse of how difficult it is to identify different types of phrases in English?"

She was as quiet as a dead, blinking her eyes, as if she was guilty of all what she had done, unintentionally. Tears were just about to roll out of her eyes. All she said was, "**I'm sorry**".

I guess I was too harsh. I was too loud. I should have been empathetic about the fact that after all she was just a kid and will now have to face all these challenges too.

Just then my maid's daughter, who was around eleven, entered my room. Well, she didn't have to study, she didn't have to toil with projects, she didn't even go to school. She just went lolling around whole day, gallivanting, to the garden, eating strawberries, having cool drinks from the nearby store.

Now, whenever I look at her, I feel

Pandora's sorry was fake. She has put all of us in trouble and she has a gala time... All the time. I wished one or two book worms would've stung her too.

www.ingramcontent.com/pod-product-compliance
Lightning Source LLC
LaVergne TN
LVHW021156160826
845679LV00024B/2142

* 9 7 9 8 8 9 2 7 7 3 8 8 1 *